How to more

The Timpson Way

First published in 2005 by Timpson Limited. © John Timpson 2005.

ISBN 0-9547049-3-2

Timpson House Claverton Road Wythenshawe Manchester M23 9TT
Tel: 0161 946 6200 www.timpson.com
Written by John Timpson CBE. Printed in Great Britain.

What's your life like?

Here is a simple way to reveal your work life balance.

1. Draw a circle with eight segments on a blank piece of paper.

2. Write 'work' in one segment, in the rest add your other seven most time consuming activities.

3. On the line to the left of each segment indicate the proportion of your time spent on the relevant activity.

4. Join up the lines.

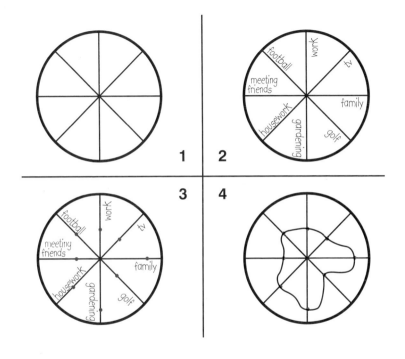

1

2

3

4

A lifetime test

Moment of truth

Compare your chart with this guide –
makes you think doesn't it?

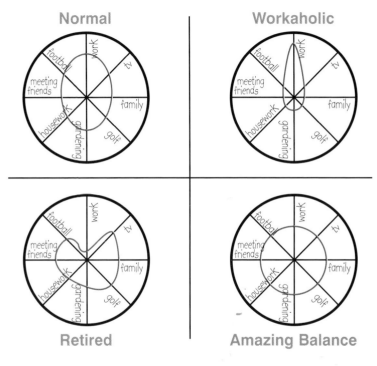

Guide to your results

Magic Formula

The next few pages reveal the secret formula for escaping the workplace treadmill.

The big secret

Turnover a new leaf

If you yearn for an easier life, read on...

Have faith in others

Trust people. Trust your boss, your colleagues and particularly your team. You can't do everything yourself, create time by giving others authority.

Trust

Delegate Authority

Management is most effective when it is turned upside down, creating time by giving your team the authority to make decisions.

Upside-down Management

Carry the can

'Upside down Management' doesn't allow you to opt out, you delegate authority but retain responsibility. You still carry the can but have created the time to keep on top of your own job.

Retain responsibility

Don't be a dictator

There are do's and don'ts of delegation. Don't issue orders, give helpful guidelines. Be realistic, don't send someone on a hopeless mission.

Delegate for success

Power of persuasion

Don't be a hard task master, support your team,
life is a lot easier if you praise and encourage,
issuing orders takes up too much time.

Don't ask me it's your decision!
Don't blame me if it doesn't work!
What on earth are you doing!
How can I explain that to the Chairman!
BAD BOSS
How's it going?
Let's do that together.
Don't worry.
Well done!
GOOD BOSS

Route One

Don't make your life complicated, it's the simple things that make money. Common sense creates more success than intricate business plans.

Keep it simple

What you're here for

Be clear what is expected of you when you turn up for work, not just what you do but what people hope you will achieve.

KEY TASKS?
~~~~~~~~~~~~~~~~~~
~~~~~~~~~~~~~~~~~~
~~~~~~~~~~~~~~~~~
~~~~~~~~~~~~~~~~~~

KEY RESULTS?
~~~~~~~~~~~~~~~~~~
~~~~~~~~~~~~~~~~~~
~~~~~~~~~~~~~~~~~~
~~~~~~~~~~~~~~~~~~

TIMPSON

What is your job?

Priorities

The example shows the difference between key tasks and signs of success. Analyse your own job in the same way.

Football Manager

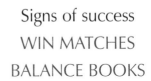

Signs of success
WIN MATCHES
BALANCE BOOKS

Key Tasks
PICK PLAYERS
ESTABLISH TACTICS
KEEP TEAM HAPPY
TALK TO PRESS

A good example

Stick to your task

Be single minded, do one job at a time and resist interruptions. Some people waste time poking their nose into other people's business.

TIP DON'T BOTHER ABOUT OTHER PEOPLE'S BUSINESS - YOU'RE NOT PAID FOR THAT.

Concentrate on the job at hand

Home Foundation

If good people go off the boil, it's usually due
to a problem outside work, often at home.
Everyone needs a good home, family and leisure
life. We like personalities who know how to
balance their lives.

Your life balance is important

What matters most

Indulge in a minute of self-analysis, who or what are most important in your life. Don't cheat, be honest with yourself.

Who or what means most to you

YOURSELF

PARTNER

KIDS

PETS

FOOTBALL

GOLF

CAR

OFFICE

MUM & DAD

PUB

TV

OTHER?

Home sweet home

What dominates your life, is it home or work, fishing or family holidays, Manchester City or your Mother in Law? Most happy people plan their lives around their home and family, work takes second place.

Plan your life around home not work

Forward Thinking

Don't be frightened of your diary, planning ahead won't wish your life away, it helps create more time.

The life control device

Face the music

Everyone has some unpleasant jobs. No one likes disciplinary interviews or telling someone they have lost their job. It's a horrible thing to do, but don't put off the inevitable, you can waste a lot of time turning over the thought of a tricky task in your mind, it is much better to tackle unwelcome jobs quickly.

Tackle unwelcome jobs quickly

Use your strengths

Don't spend time doing jobs you find difficult when other people can do the task quicker and better. Accept your limitations and concentrate on what you are good at, it will save you time.

PERSONAL ASSESSMENT	
D.I.Y	✓
ADMIN	✗
IDEAS	✓
PEOPLE	✓
MEETINGS	✗
PLANNING	✓
COMPUTERS	✗
DISPLAY	✗

Know your strengths

Stand Back

Be a Manager and give your people the space to learn. You are bound to be better at some tasks than members of your team, but don't do their job for them.

Don't invade your people's jobs

Don't Brood

Worry wastes lots of time, if you have a problem don't let it fester, talk about it. Don't just talk to your boss, unburden your nagging thoughts on anyone else you trust.

Don't worry on your own

Leave it to them

Control freaks never relax, they always agonise about business. Trust your team to take chances and make mistakes but still accept responsibility on their behalf.

Trust your colleagues

Don't be a mug

You can't please all your people all of the time. Learn to say no and avoid the risk of spending your time on monotonous tasks.

Think First

Don't fill your diary full of other people's problems. Think carefully before volunteering your personal commitment. It's easy to accept a new challenge but you may be offering a slice of time you can ill afford.

Don't take on more than you can handle

Fools rush in

Some chance remarks can come back to haunt you, only make promises you have the ability and time to keep.

Don't make vague promises

Don't be a hero

Don't volunteer unless you desperately want the task and have the time to do it.

Think before you speak

Overwhelmed

If you are fire fighting an overwhelming list of problems, it's time to reorganise your life. Some of the ideas in this book should help. If you are still fire fighting in four months time, you are in the wrong job.

Avoid firefighting

Is the meeting worth your time?

Treat meetings as optional, only turn up if they are worth your time. Remember, it only takes five minutes to read the notes from a three hour meeting.

Early Bath

Don't try to be superman, it's the extra visit beyond the call of duty that makes you late home. Be sensible and if possible beat the rush hour.

A shop too far!

Clear Conscience

Don't feel guilty about thinking time.
Creative thinking is really valuable, find
the peace and quiet to do it.

Create time to think

Mr Overkeen

Some people crave the attention of senior management hoping to secure promotion through conspicuous hard work – first to arrive in the morning and last to leave the office each night, they volunteer for everything and never miss a meeting.

But overwork is no guarantee of success, they usually only succeed in getting up the bosses nose.

Silly superman

Meddling Managers

Some managers never let you off the leash,
they always look over your shoulder to make
sure you don't make a mistake. They are so
busy micro-managing, they haven't time to
do their own job.

Won't let go

Helpful Guidance

Delegation isn't about telling people what to do, that's what a Dictator does. Good managers delegate objectives and provide the freedom to achieve them. They give help, not instruction, that's 'Upside down Management.'

Computer Clown

Only shallow minded managers brag about how much work they do. Smart operators concentrate on things that really matter.

Tedious Talk

Try to contact some people and they are always in a meeting, but are they doing their job? I have noticed successful companies have fewer meetings and are good at communication. Many meetings waste time and have participants with a personal political agenda.

Road Hog

Don't measure success by the number of miles you drive, you can't do good business stuck behind a desk, but you shouldn't spend all your time driving 75 m.p.h. down a motorway.

Motorway maniacs

Nightwatchman

Don't be impressed by the person who always works late at the office. Being the last to leave often identifies someone who can't manage their time.

Last to go home

Plan Ahead

Take control of your life by planning your diary, some things never get done unless you make a firm commitment. This doesn't just apply to the business, also plan your home life.

Make time to plan

Big Planner

A three month planner can help you get more
out of your life. Follow the guidelines on the
next few pages.

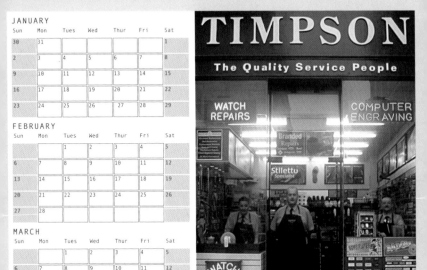

Use a big picture planner

Fixed Points

Put in all the fixed events – Area Meetings,
birthdays, holidays, anniversaries, conferences.

10	11	12	1

16	17	18 CONFERENCE	19	2

23	24 AREA MEETING	25	26	

FEBRUARY

Sun	Mon	Tues	Wed	T
		1 ANNE'S BIRTHDAY	2	3
6	7	8	9	1

Put in known events

| | | | | 1 |

Home Agenda

Add your personal plans, days off, football matches, DIY, medical appointments and golf, making sure it all fits in with your partner's diary.

26	27	28	29

Wed	Thur	Fri	Sat
2	3	4	5 GOLF TRIP (Hurray!)
9 NEW KITCHEN	10	11	12
16	17	18	19

2

Add family and personal

Job Planning

Add your business programme, branch visits, other meetings, discussion groups, thinking days, but don't fill up every hour of every day, leave plenty of time to wander round talking to your team.

	on	Tues	Wed	Thur	Fr
		1	2 BRANCH VISITS	3	4
	7	8	9	10	11
	14	15 TRIBUNAL	16	17	18
	21.	22	23	24	25

Add your business plan

Set in stone

Transfer the three months' plan into your diary or personal organiser, if you don't keep a proper diary, start right now.

Transfer to diary

Monthly Focus

Set your three main team objectives for the months ahead. If everyone goes for the same small number of goals together you will make a difference.

1 Skill Tests
2 Watch Training
3 House-keeping

Agree top tasks

Red letter days

Enter all pre-determined events in your plan.

List known events

Individual Agenda

Get every member of your team to draw up their plan. In 'Upside down Management' individuals decide how to allocate their own time.

Get everyone to plan

Realism

No plan can turn you into a superman. Use common sense when setting your programme, only cover 40 hours work a week.

Be realistic

Unite the plans

Put all the individual plans together ready
for a team debate.

Compare notes

The debate

Talk about all the major issues – and discuss every shop to identify any significant problems.

Be honest with each other, it saves a lot of time.

Frank discussion

Five week plan

Every area team should have a five week plan to provide a focal point, it stimulates delegation, communication, co-ordination and sets the objectives. Make sure everyone owns your five week plan.

	DATES	A.WILLINGHAM	P.DUCKERS	R.COOLEY	M.JONES	V.SPURDLE
		A.W	P.D	R.C	M.J	V.S
MONDAY	21/06/2004	ADM MEET	ADM MEET	ADM MEET	ADM MEET	ADM MEET
TUESDAY	22/06/2004	731	D/O	D/O	72	748
WEDNESDAY	23/06/2004	272	784	731	D/O	748
THURSDAY	24/06/2004	124	272	834	124	140
FRIDAY	25/06/2004	D/OWED	272	748	196	D/O
SATURDAY	26/06/2004	D/O	272	748	D/O	300
SUNDAY	27/06/2004					
		A.W	P.D	R.C	M.J	V.S
MONDAY	28/06/2004	748/746	72	272	196	196
TUESDAY	29/06/2004	300/196	287	746	834	72
WEDNESDAY	30/06/2004	731	731	462/196/072/300	D/O	300
THURSDAY	01/07/2004	731	731	140	148	591
FRIDAY	02/07/2004	490	139	124	300	D/O
SATURDAY	03/07/2004	D/O	D/O	D/O	AREA	AREA
SUNDAY	04/07/2004					
		A.W	P.D	R.C	M.J	V.S
MONDAY	05/07/2004	124	72	784	834	139
TUESDAY	06/07/2004	287	196	748/809	881	748
WEDNESDAY	07/07/2004	D/O	140	DEXTORS	843	140
THURSDAY	08/07/2004	287	WITH D.PHILLIPS	DEXTORS	124	D/O
FRIDAY	09/07/2004	287	124	748/072	D/O	140
SATURDAY	10/07/2004	287	D/O	D/O	748	140
SUNDAY	11/07/2004					
		A.W	P.D	R.C	M.J	V.S
MONDAY	12/07/2004	287	72	809	287	287
TUESDAY	13/07/2004	140	480/196	809	140	809
WEDNESDAY	14/07/2004	DEXTORS	786	124	124	INTERVIEWS
THURSDAY	15/07/2004	72	124	124	124	124
FRIDAY	16/07/2004	D/O	D/O	809	586	124
SATURDAY	17/07/2004	140	272	809	986	D/O
SUNDAY	18/07/2004					
		A.W	P.D	R.C	M.J	V.S
MONDAY	19/07/2004	683	784	868	287	809
TUESDAY	20/07/2004	190	462	866	834	809
WEDNESDAY	21/07/2004	834	806	D/O	D/O	287
THURSDAY	22/07/2004	784	586	124	140	809
FRIDAY	23/07/2004	124	809	138	300	D/O
SATURDAY	24/07/2004	D/O	D/O	139	AREA	809
SUNDAY	25/07/2004					
NEXT A.D.M. MEETING		26.07.04				

Finished product

Make a difference

Revise the plans in response to your discussion. Decisions that involve people matter most because it's people that make the difference.

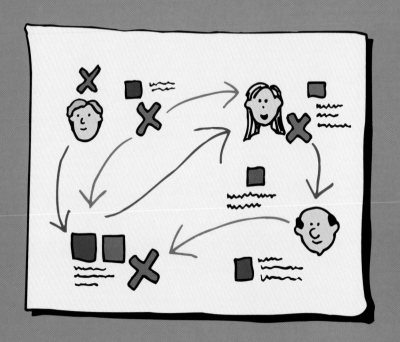

Decision time

Clear Direction

Everyone now has their plan for the next five weeks - let them get on with it.

	DATES	A.WILLINGHAM	P.DUCKERS	R.COOLEY	M.JONES	V.SPURDLE
		A.W	P.D	R.C	M.J	V.S
MONDAY	21/06/2004	ADM MEET	ADM MEET	ADM MEET	ADM MEET	ADM MEET
TUESDAY	22/06/2004	745	748/809	D/O	72	745
WEDNESDAY	23/06/2004	462/190/072/300	DEXTORS	731	D/O	745
THURSDAY	24/06/2004	140	DEXTORS	834	124	140
FRIDAY	25/06/2004	124	748/072	745	196	D/O
SATURDAY	26/06/2004	D/O	D/O	745	D/O	300
SUNDAY	27/06/2004					
		A.W	P.D	R.C	M.J	V.S
MONDAY	28/06/2004	748/745	72	272	196	196
TUESDAY	29/06/2004	300/196	287	D/O	834	72
WEDNESDAY	30/06/2004	731	731	784	D/O	300
THURSDAY	01/07/2004	731	731	272	140	591
FRIDAY	02/07/2004	490	139	272	300	D/O
SATURDAY	03/07/2004	D/O	D/O	272	AREA	AREA
SUNDAY	04/07/2004					
		A.W	P.D	R.C	M.J	V.S
MONDAY	05/07/2004	124	72	784	834	139
TUESDAY	06/07/2004	196	140	784	591	745
WEDNESDAY	07/07/2004	140	DEXTORS	784	843	140
THURSDAY	08/07/2004	WITH D.PHILLIPS	72	Dextors	124	D/O
FRIDAY	09/07/2004	124	D/O	784	D/O	140
SATURDAY	10/07/2004	D/O	140	D/O	748	140
SUNDAY	11/07/2004					
		A.W	P.D	R.C	M.J	V.S
MONDAY	12/07/2004	287	72	809	287	287
TUESDAY	13/07/2004	809	490/196	809	140	731
WEDNESDAY	14/07/2004	INTERVIEWS	796	D/O	D/O	272
THURSDAY	15/07/2004	124	124	124	124	124
FRIDAY	16/07/2004	124	D/O	809	586	D/OWED
SATURDAY	17/07/2004	D/O	272	809	866	D/O
SUNDAY	18/07/2004					
		A.W	P.D	R.C	M.J	V.S
MONDAY	19/07/2004	583	784	866	287	809
TUESDAY	20/07/2004	196	462	866	287	809
WEDNESDAY	21/07/2004	834	806	D/O	D/O	287
THURSDAY	22/07/2004	784	585	139	287	809
FRIDAY	23/07/2004	124	809	139	287	D/O
SATURDAY	24/07/2004	D/O	D/O	139	287	809
SUNDAY	25/07/2004					
NEXT A.D.M. MEETING		26.07.04				

Sorted!

Be Prepared

Save time by building your own personal reference library. Find a way to keep day-to-day facts at your fingertips.

Useful info on hand

Know How

Experience saves time. The more you know about the business, the quicker your job will become.

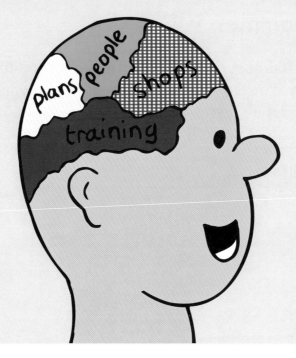

Know the business

Chairman's Duty

As Chairman of a meeting you are responsible for making use of the time spent by everyone round the table.

With poor Chairmanship, meetings become a complete waste of time.

Running a meeting

Reasons to meet

Before fixing the date think what the meeting is for.

Meetings fall into three categories:

1. Brainstorming (search for views and ideas.)

2. Discussion.

3. Communication.

Never make a decision at a meeting.

If you doubt the value of any meeting, cancel it.

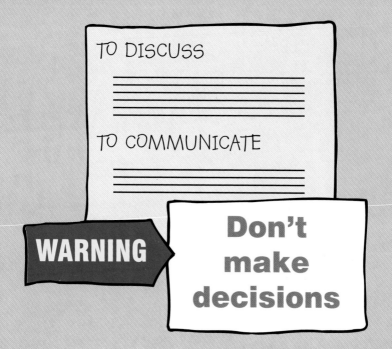

The Agenda

Meetings must have discipline. An agenda keeps you to the point.

Control document

Prompt Papers

Give people plenty of time to read papers before the meeting.

Early reports

Timekeeping

Ignore latecomers and start on time –
always finish early.

Start on time - finish early

Signs of a good chairman

1. STICK TO THE POINT

> Very interesting, but can I bring you back to our capital expenditure plans.

2. CUT OUT CACKLING

> I know you have strong views but we must move on.

How do **YOU** see it Tony?

We are generally agreed to expand jewellery repairs and ask James to finalise his plan before our next meeting.

Conference Characters

A good Chairman knows the characters round the table. Some need encouragement, others must be kept quiet.

Here are a few of the people you are likely to meet.

Spot the difference

Selfish, always looking to further his own importance even at the expense of others.

Political Pete

Full of ideas but lacks the courage to speak.

Shy Susan

For Pat, procedure is more important than content, he wants to trip you up.

Procedural Pat

Little things that can save a lot of time

Some people create time by keeping their lives uncomplicated, here are a few of the things they do:

Time saving tips

Without Delay

The easiest and quickest way is to do a job straight away.

Do it now

Early Start

Calm, unflappable people start early in the morning, tackle their jobs first thing and enjoy the rest of the day.

Start early - finish early

Persevere

Follow the phrase, 'I've started so I'll finish.'

It is worth working late occasionally to finish a job, but reward yourself with some time off the following day.

Finish the job

Changing Times

Don't be a creature of habit, work the hours that help you get the job done when you want to do it.

Flexitime

Plot Ahead

The time to look at a map is the night before your journey.

Traffic planning

Make a list

Put your tasks on a list, as you get older your memory fades, but the list comes to your rescue - as long as you remember where you put it.

Ring Bob
Wrexham display
Car service
Hair cut
John's birthday
Wedding anniversary

Write it down

Squanderers

When you start a new job, you have loads of time, you haven't been sucked into the Company clutter and office gossip. You won't escape for long, here are some of the big time wasters –

Timewasters

Mammoth Memos

Long reports could have been written in a fraction of the time and are seldom worth reading. The best memos stick to one page and stick to the point.

DETAILED REPORT
ON JOINED UP
ADMINISTRATION

(Volume One)

Long reports

Costly Conventions

Some say conferences broaden the mind and provide a networking opportunity, but few conferences offer value for money. Don't be tempted to spend two days and £650.00 watching people present their carefully prepared prose on PowerPoint.

THE IMPORTANCE OF
POWERPOINT
PRESENTATIONS

PART 3

Conferences

Sub Groups

Working parties are a cop out, set up by individuals who can't make up their minds.

When a working party meets more than once, it could go on forever and is in danger of giving birth to more working parties.

Working parties

Cut the circulation

Some executives have a pile of unread magazines in their office and are guilty they haven't found time to keep up-do-date with industry news. There is a solution, put the magazines in the skip.

Trade magazines

Cancel Fridays

Save hours every week by working at home on a Friday, never tackle the motorways on Friday afternoon.

Travelling on a Friday

Administrative Burden

Do you have to trudge through a mound of paperwork and emails before you can start your real job? Do you feel guilty if you don't do justice to your incoming mail? Do you feel some of your colleagues bombard you with communications that make life difficult? The answer to your problem is in the next few pages.

Only Once

Nothing deserves to be read more than once, if you can't understand it first time, it's either badly written or above your head.

Make a firm rule, only read things once.

TIP
BIN THE RUBBISH

IN

OUT

Instant decision

Short Cut

If you receive a long report, only read the introduction and conclusion, they will tell you all you need to know.

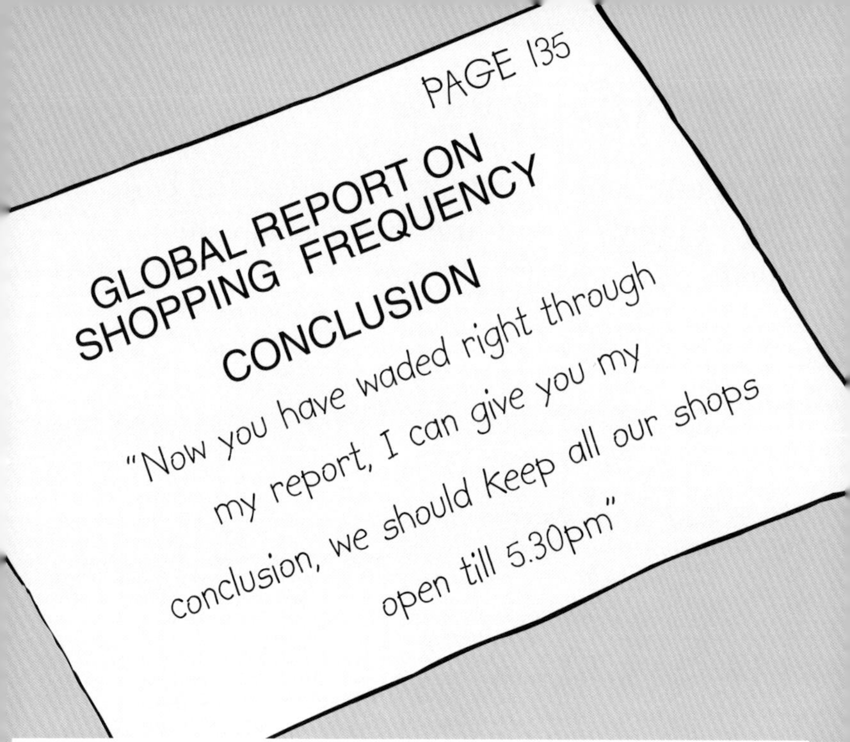

Go straight to the summary

Quick Response

Don't be seduced into a memo war, the best way to reply is to return the original with a written comment.

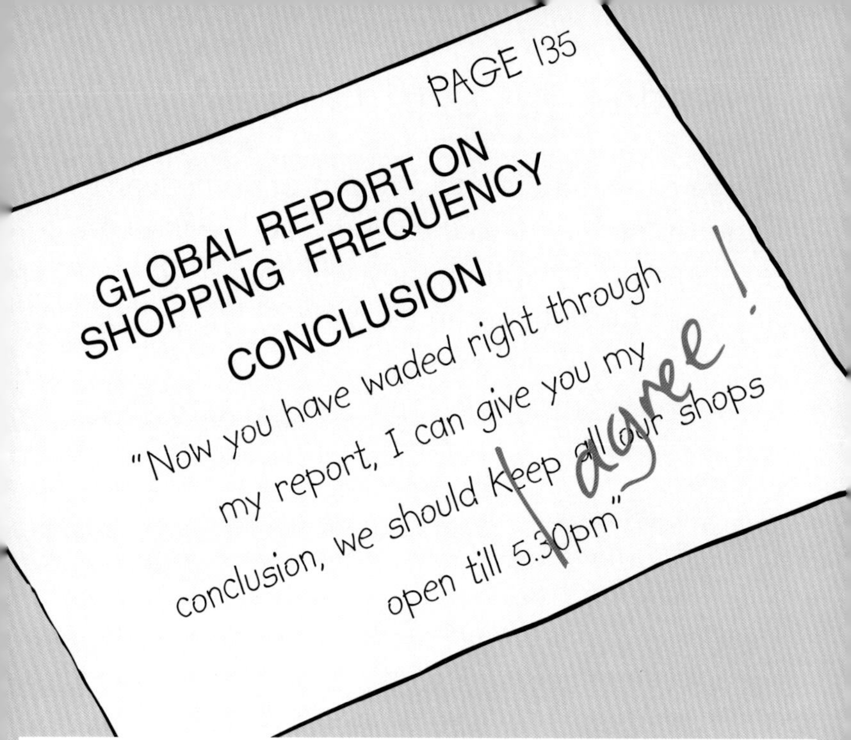

Short pointed reply

Demand an explanation

If you can't understand a report or you haven't time to read it, go to the sender and request an explanation. Next time they will come and chat instead of producing an essay.

Get off the list

Take pride in the small size of your post bag, get off as many mailing lists as you can.

VERY IMPORTANT

REFIT ANALYSIS

SHOP No 367

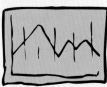

Please don't send me this report again!

Cut the circulation

Not worth keeping

When you have read it once, throw it away, don't file memos and circulars, if you ever need to see them again, most of the other people in your office will have a copy on file.

Don't file it

Chuck It

You are faced with a choice with every memo you receive:

> **Either** 1 - *read it and throw it away.*

> **Or...** 2 - *throw it away without reading it.*

Get a big waste paper basket and use it regularly.

Bin it

I.T. Myth

Most of us are still nervous of I.T. We think computer illiteracy is a sign of age or incompetence and are willing to bow to I.T.'s better judgement.

Don't be fooled, the I.T. industry still has a lot to learn and we are their guinea pigs – a lot of things to do with I.T. are expensive and time consuming.

Here are a few tips to avoid the traps:

Ban email circulars

As soon as you send emails and open your in box, you start receiving copies of some of the most boring messages ever seen. "My revised holiday dates are." "The shredder man is coming." "Has anyone seen my pen?" All these appeared in my In Box during January. So I took action, "Please exclude me from your email circulation." It worked, my emails reduced by 80%.

A small number of people think they are so interesting they copy their emails to everyone who has a computer. Keep off their mailing list.

Come off the list

Keep Quiet

Computers, mobile 'phones and other devices like the Blackberry should be mute whenever possible.

You don't want messages that makes a noisy interruption when you have real work to do.

Pet Hate

I HATE VOICE MAIL,

I HATE VOICE MAIL,

I HATE VOICE MAIL!

Because it inconveniences the caller for the benefit of the receiver. It's rude and it wastes time.

Time waster

Give the message

Whenever you have to speak to business voice mail, you have every right to feel insulted.

Leave a message that makes your point.

Dealing with voice mail

Real People

When someone rings Timpson, they will have a real person at the other end of the line.

Gossip Game

Other people can waste a lot of your time by talking too much – learn how to bring conversations to an end without causing offence.

10 ways to end a conversation

5 ways to end a conversation

"There's someone at the door."

"I've got a urgent appointment."

"I agree with you."

"It doesn't matter what you say the answer is no."

"Gosh is that the time."

5 more ways to end a conversation

"Have you seen the traffic."

"I've really enjoyed our meeting."

"My wife is arriving any moment."

"Where are you going now."

"I'm five minutes late for my next meeting."

Home Study

Home is a good place to work as long as you maintain a clear divide between business and pleasure.

Working at home

Routine

Set yourself a strict routine – start and finish on time and take a planned break for lunch. Make sure your family respect the timetable.

Strict timetable

Territory

Establish your work space. You and the family will soon grow accustomed to the bit of your house called the office.

Specified place

Isolation

If you want your work to be effective, keep away from your partner, children and the television until the job has been done.

 TV

 KIDS

 PARTNER

AVOID!

Beware the 'phone

Do business on your mobile and never answer the home 'phone unless you want to become your partner's secretary.

Don't answer

Give it a rest

Plan some breaks during the day and take them away from your work space

Take a break

Watch the clock

It's easy to put in overtime at home, but it could turn you into a workaholic. Don't work late, your family expect you to adopt your home role on time.

Finish on time

Change your habit

Mark the end of work by tidying away your papers, having a shower and changing into more casual clothes.

Have a shower & change

Relax

Some people find it easy to switch off, others always appear eager and tense. Whatever your personality, there are things you can do to make life more relaxed.

Sit down lunch

Don't be a snacker, a coke and a packet of crisps isn't good enough. Sit down and take a break.

Have a proper lunch

Diversion

Give yourself a rest and switch off your mobile, if a call is really important they will leave a message.

Switch off

Who Cares?

Worry takes lots of time and energy but achieves nothing. Find a way to replace pessimistic brooding with positive thinking.

Do something not work related

Trouble Shared

If you can't get something off your mind –
talk about it.

Think Leisure

Have plenty of interests that take your mind away from work. Read a book, play the piano, or do a crossword, too much work makes you boring.

Outside interests

Real Interest

Do you have a real hobby? That does not include watching television and going out at night. If you haven't got a hobby, why not? Did I hear you say you haven't got the time?

Have an absorbing hobby

Activity

Exercise is a great way to unwind, it clears the mind and keeps you fit. How many times a week do you take over half an hour's active exercise?

Physical exercise

Vacation

Take holidays seriously. They are the most important weeks of the year. Choose trips you look forward to, anticipation is a big part of the pleasure.

Holidays

Create a deadline

The world is split between people who get things done before they go on holiday and those who delay everything until they return.

Use your holiday as a deadline and be one of those that get things done. Before you go away make sure your desk is clear of all current problems.

You have to get it done before I go!

A good excuse

Finish all current jobs.

Clear the decks

Don't start any new jobs

Memory Pad

List all your outstanding tasks before you leave so you can pick up the thread quickly on your return.

JOHN'S BIG LIST
Training manual
"Create More Time" book
Watch repair display
AM's conference
Jewellery repairs
ChildLine appeal

List your current priorities

Dare to delegate

Give your team the authority to deal with everything while you are away. You are not indispensable.

Delegate everything

Welcome Back

Ask your regular contacts to write a short report on events ready for your return. They will help you rejoin the team without losing the plot.

Ask for a short report on your return

On Leave

A holiday is not a holiday if you think about work talk about work or do any work, your job is to be 100% on holiday.

During the holiday

No Paperwork

Leave your briefcase behind and don't cheat by hiding paperwork in your suitcase.

No briefcase!

Switch Off

Lock your mobile and put it in a drawer, don't be tempted to look up emails and if you have a Blackberry leave it at home.

Put your mobile in a drawer

Holiday Reading

Take plenty of books, but only one business book.
On second thoughts leave the business book
behind, most of them are boring.

Have plenty to read

Office Dreaming

If your mind starts to wander towards work, change the subject. If you are desperately needed by the office, they will find you, so no news is good news.

Forget about it

Re-entry

Going back to work is the toughest part of every holiday. Be prepared for three days walking in a daze.

Back to work

Warm Up

Don't charge in at 100 miles an hour, you need to work up gently to your normal pace. If you jump straight in, you lose much of the benefit of your holiday.

Take it easy

Socialise

Spend time getting up-to-date. Meet as many people as possible – catch up with the business news and the gossip.

Look at your job with a fresh pair of eyes.

TIP TREAT IT LIKE STARTING A NEW JOB

Meet everyone

Rejoin the agenda

Get out the list you made before your holiday and decide what you want to do first.

John's Big Li...

Training manual
"Create More Time" book
Watch repair display
AM's conference
Jewellery repairs
ChildLine appeal

Look at your list

Visit the travel agent

Before becoming totally immersed in work again, book your next holiday, you always need something to look forward to.

Book your next holiday

Progress Report

This book has lots of ideas to help you create more spare time and take charge of your work life balance. But how well are you doing? The last few pages provide you with a progress report, but don't cheat, it's your life you are playing with.

THE
TRUTH

Reality check

Honesty Check

Use this daily pad to check whether your
time is well spent.

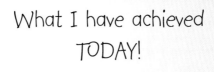

What I have achieved
TODAY!

Wrote 30 well done letters
Fixed Tuscany holiday
Beat Gordon at golf
Visited 3 shops
Caught Stuart on the phone

I deserve some time off!

Achievement pad

Time Sheet

How many hours did you work last week – fill in this chart to find the answer.

My working week

	START	FINISH	HOURS
M			
T			
W			
T			
F			
S			
S			
		TOTAL	

Time sheet

Confession

Can you summon the courage to be really honest? Will you confess to doing things you shouldn't do or need not do? Why work on things that aren't your job?

Be really honest with yourself

Life's rich pattern

Remember that chart at the beginning, have another go to see if you have changed the shape of your life.

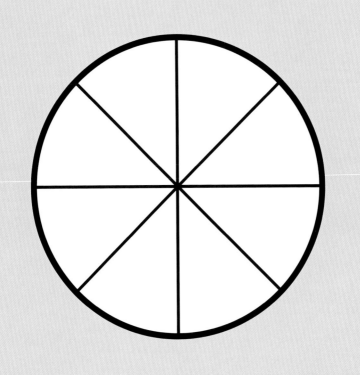